I0421749

THIS JOURNAL BELONGS TO:

____

www.ingramcontent.com/pod-product-compliance
Lightning Source LLC
Chambersburg PA
CBHW070420290526
45791CB00005B/1763